of Congress Cataloging–in–Publication Data

tion to financial accounting: a user perspective/Kumen H.
. . . [et al.].
cm.
ludes bibliographical references and index.
BN 0-13-228768-4
Accounting   2. Financial statements.   I. Jones, Kumen H.
635.I657 1996   95-6526
dc20   CIP

uisitions Editor: *Rob Dewey*
tor in Chief: *Richard Wohl*
sistant Editor: *Diane DeCastro*
velopment Editor: *David Cohen*
litor in Chief, Development: *Stephen Deitmer*
roduction Editor: *Edith Pullman*
nterior Design: *Delgado Design, Inc.*
Design Director: *Patricia H. Wosczyk*
Photo Research: *Teri Stratford*
Photo Coordinator: *Melinda Reo*
Prepress and Manufacturing Buyer: *Paul Smolenski*
Production Services Manager: *Lorraine Patsco*
Electronic Page Layout: *Christy Mahon*
Electronic Artist: *Warren Fischbach*
Cover Art: *Marjory Dressler/Photo-Graphics*

FASB Concepts Statements No. 1, *Objectives of Financial Reporting by Business Enterprises,* No. 2, *Qualitative Characteristics of Accounting Information,* and No. 6, *Elements of Financial Statements,* are copyrighted by the Financial Accounting Standards Board, 401 Merritt 7, P.O. Box 5116, Norwalk, Connecticut, 06856-5116, U.S.A. Portions are reprinted with permission. Copies of the complete documents are available from the FASB.

Quotations in Chapters 3, 10, and 13 from American Institute of Certified Public Accountants are Copyright ©1994 by American Institute of Certified Public Accountants, Inc. Reprinted with permission.

The authors dedicate this book
to their families.

ISBN 0-13-228768-4 (Student Edition)
ISBN 0-13-228776-5 (Instructor Edition)

Prentice-Hall International (UK) Limited, *London*
Prentice-Hall of Australia Pty. Limited, *Sydney*
Prentice-Hall Canada Inc., *Toronto*
Prentice-Hall Hispanoamericana, S.A., *Mexico*
Prentice-Hall of India Private Limited, *New Delhi*
Prentice-Hall of Japan, Inc., *Tokyo*
Simon & Schuster Asia Pte. Ltd., *Singapore*
Editora Prentice-Hall do Brasil, Ltda., *Rio de Janeiro*

Introduction to Financial Accounting

A User Perspective

Kumen H. Jones
Arizona State University

Jean B. Price
Clemson University

Michael L. Werner
University of Miami

Martha S. Doran
Stephens College

 Prentice Hall, Englewood Cliffs, New Jersey 07632

Brief Contents

Contents